Life Skills

Managing Money

by Emma Huddleston

FOCUS READERS®
PIONEER

www.focusreaders.com

Copyright © 2021 by Focus Readers®, Lake Elmo, MN 55042. All rights reserved. No part of this book may be reproduced or utilized in any form or by any means without written permission from the publisher.

Focus Readers is distributed by North Star Editions:
sales@northstareditions.com | 888-417-0195

Produced for Focus Readers by Red Line Editorial.

Photographs ©: iStockphoto, cover, 1, 4, 7, 8, 12, 15 (tickets, suitcase, bear), 16, 19; Shutterstock Images, 11, 15 (house, dress, watch); Red Line Editorial, 21

Library of Congress Cataloging-in-Publication Data
Names: Huddleston, Emma, author.
Title: Managing money / Emma Huddleston.
Description: Lake Elmo : Focus Readers, 2021. | Series: Life skills |
    Includes index. | Audience: Grades 2–3
Identifiers: LCCN 2019057411 (print) | LCCN 2019057412 (ebook) | ISBN
    9781644933442 (hardcover) | ISBN 9781644934203 (paperback) | ISBN
    9781644935729 (pdf) | ISBN 9781644934968 (ebook)
Subjects: LCSH: Finance, Personal--Juvenile literature. | Budget--Juvenile
    literature.
Classification: LCC HG179 .H83 2021 (print) | LCC HG179 (ebook) | DDC
    332.024--dc23
LC record available at https://lccn.loc.gov/2019057411
LC ebook record available at https://lccn.loc.gov/2019057412

Printed in the United States of America
Mankato, MN
082020

About the Author

Emma Huddleston lives in the Twin Cities with her husband. Her favorite part about managing money is saving for vacations with her family.

Table of Contents

CHAPTER 1
What Is Money? 5

CHAPTER 2
Earning Money 9

CHAPTER 3
Spending or Saving 13

CHAPTER 4
Setting a Budget 17

Make a Budget 20

Focus on Managing Money • 22
Glossary • 23
To Learn More • 24
Index • 24

Chapter 1

What Is Money?

Money is anything people can use to pay for things. Money can be metal coins or paper bills. Each piece of money has a value.

People can use money to buy **goods**. Goods include books and clothing. People can also use money to pay for **services**. Services include haircuts and visits to the doctor.

Fun Fact

Different countries use different kinds of money. The United States uses the dollar. Many countries in Europe use the euro.

Chapter 2

Earning Money

People earn money by working. They do a job. Then they get paid for their work. People can do many kinds of work.

Some jobs include doing a service for others. For example, pilots fly planes. Teachers teach students.

Other jobs include making and selling goods. For example, painters make art. Factory workers make objects such as bicycles or soap. People can **spend** or **save** the money they earn.

Chapter 3

Spending or Saving

People can spend money on needs or wants. Needs are things people must have to live. Wants are things people enjoy.

Some objects cost more money than others. A house costs more than a meal. A vacation costs more than a toy. People need to save money to **afford** more costly items.

Fun Fact — Some people save their money in a **bank**.

Needs and Wants

Needs
- food
- housing
- clothing

Wants
- toys
- jewelry
- candy
- video games
- vacations

15

Chapter 4

Setting a Budget

People can use a **budget** to track their money. People see how much they earn. They also see how much they spend or save.

People should buy what they need first. Then they can decide how to use the rest of their money. People may need to save for what they want. People shouldn't spend more money than they earn.

Try It Out!

Make a Budget

Write your own budget! Use a budget to track the money you earn, spend, and save.

1. How much money do you earn?

2. What do you want or need? How much do those things cost?

3. Is there anything you can buy right away? Or do you need to save money first?

Source of Money	Amount
Allowance	
Job	
Gift	
Other: _____	
Other: _____	
Total	

Things I Want or Need	Cost of Item	Can I Buy This Now?
Toy/Game		Yes/No
Clothing/ Shoes		Yes/No
Movie/Activity		Yes/No
Candy/Treat		Yes/No
Other: _____		Yes/No
Other: _____		Yes/No

FOCUS ON
Managing Money

Write your answers on a separate piece of paper.

1. Write a sentence describing how people can earn money.

2. Why do you think saving money is important?

3. What is an example of a need?
   A. a candy bar
   B. a place to live
   C. a video game

4. How does a budget help people manage money?
   A. It helps people make sure they aren't spending more than they earn.
   B. It helps people keep their money in a safe place.
   C. It helps people earn money for doing jobs.

Answer key on page 24.

Glossary

afford
To have enough money to pay for something.

bank
A place that keeps people's money safe.

budget
A tool that helps people keep track of how much they save and spend.

goods
Items people can buy.

save
To set money aside so it can be used later.

services
Actions of helping or doing work for others.

spend
To use money to pay for something.

To Learn More

BOOKS

Gaertner, Meg. *Spending and Saving Money.* Minneapolis: Pop!, 2018.

Sherman, Jill. *Money: What You Need to Know.* North Mankato, MN: Capstone Press, 2017.

NOTE TO EDUCATORS

Visit **www.focusreaders.com** to find lesson plans, activities, links, and other resources related to this title.

Index

B
budget, 17, 20

G
goods, 6, 10

J
jobs, 9–10, 21

S
save, 10, 14, 17–18, 20
services, 6, 10
spend, 10, 13, 17–18, 20

Answer Key: 1. Answers will vary; **2.** Answers will vary; **3.** B; **4.** A